Your Amazing Itty Bitty® Relationships as a Spiritual Practice

15 ways to Experience Relationships as a Heartfelt Loving Adventure

Relationships as a Spiritual Practice uses 15 spiritual truths and principles to inform you, guide you, and enlighten you as you navigate the experiences of intimacy.

In this Itty Bitty book you will learn:

- a deeper understanding of love and relationships
- what it means to be authentic and free in relationships
- the value and power of forgiveness in relationships
- how to connect to your Divine Intuitive Wisdom to inform and guide you in experiencing relationships that are loving and powerful

If you want to increase the power of your own relationship pickup a copy of this Amazing Itty Bitty Book today!

Your Amazing Itty Bitty® Relationships as a Spiritual Practice

15 ways to Experience Relationships as a Heartfelt Loving Adventure

Deborah A. Gayle

Published by Itty Bitty® Publishing
A subsidiary of S & P Productions, Inc.

Copyright © 2020 Deborah A. Gayle

All rights reserved. No part of this book may be reproduced or transmitted in any form or by any means, electronic or mechanical, including photocopying, recording or by any information storage and retrieval system, without written permission of the publisher, except for inclusion of brief quotations in a review.

Printed in the United States of America

Itty Bitty Publishing
311 Main Street, Suite D
El Segundo, CA 90245
(310) 640-8885

ISBN: 978-1-950326-33-4

I dedicate this book to my late husband Rev. Nirvana Reginald Gayle, who showed me, through the joy and pain of our relationship, how to be free.

I also dedicate this book to my daughter Irisna Gayle, who reminded me that my experiences and learnings in relationship should be shared.

Stop by our Itty Bitty® website Directory to find interesting relationship information

www.IttyBittyPublishing.com

Or visit Deborah at:

deborahagayle.com

Table of Contents

Introduction
Step 1. Relationships: Journey into Your Soul
Step 2. Begin at The Beginning: Who Do You Think You Are?
Step 3. Power in Relationships: Choice: Your Ultimate Authority
Step 4. What Is Love? Self-Discovery
Step 5. Relationships Require More Than Love: What Will You Do for Love?
Step 6. Relationships: The Inside Job
Step 7. Relationships: A Reason, A Season, A Lifetime
Step 8. What Am I Pretending Not to Know? Cosmic GPS
Step 9. Crisis: From Heartbreak to Breakthrough
Step 10. Change: Who Are We Now?
Step 11. Infidelity: You Did What?
Step 12. Forgiveness: It's All About You!
Step 13. How Do I Trust Again?
Step 14. Integrity: Your Super Power
Step 15. Standing in The Light: Being Free in Relationships and in Life

Introduction

Relationships as a Spiritual Practice uses spiritual truths and principles in fifteen steps to inform you, guide you, and enlighten you as you navigate the experiences of relationships.

Each of the fifteen steps is followed by a prayer to connect and anchor the learning in your heart, your awareness and your life.

The intention of this book is to free you from limited ideas and beliefs and allow you to experience intimate relationships as a heartfelt, loving adventure.

Step 1
Relationships: Journey into Your Soul

Relationships can activate your path toward a spiritual awakening through intimacy, opening your heart, facing heartbreak, and being in joy while sharing your life with another person.

1. Relationships are all about you. Your experiences in relationships become a mirror that reflects who you are and your beliefs.
2. Your strengths, patterns, fears, and judgments are activated when you enter a relationship. What was once hidden from your awareness comes forward for you to see, address, and heal.
3. The relationship becomes the canvas where your life experiences are painted for you to see.

Being Guided to Yourself and God

Relationships present opportunities to practice spiritual qualities such as love, forgiveness, compassion, acceptance, gratitude, bliss, trust and integrity.

- You can become a better version of yourself by surrendering and learning to live the spiritual qualities activated in relationships.
- In order to take this soul journey, you must be willing to be lovingly honest with yourself, release judgement, and be courageously present in your life as you allow yourself to grow and evolve into a person where love thrives.

In this moment I am willing to surrender the all of me to God to become the highest and best version of myself as I enter into relationship. I look lovingly and courageously at my life. I cultivate a positive, honest, and loving relationship with myself. I know I am changing and transforming daily into a person where love is vibrant and active.

Step 2
Your Truth: Begin at The Beginning

In this vast universe you are a vital and important part of creation. The power of all of the cosmos is individualized as who you are. However, you must recognize this spiritual truth to activate it in your life.

1. Just like a wave is the activity of the ocean, you are the activity of the One Power and presence known as God. You are created in Its image and likeness.
2. You are an unrepeatable idea in the universe. Your unique fingerprints are a demonstration that no one has your unique life pattern.
3. Because you are alive you have a contribution to bring to life and to everyone you meet and to everything you do.
4. You are an essential aspect of life Itself.

Who Do You Think You Are?

When you recognize and know your true identity as a unique pattern of life, you never seek to control your partner or have someone validate you. You are confident in who you really are. You give and receive love freely because you know your worth and your value.

- If you know your identity, there is a greater likelihood that you will act and behave in alignment with who you really are.
- You do not look for a relationship to define or fulfil you because you are defined and filled by knowing your divine design.

I accept and know that I am an unrepeatable idea in the mind of God. I acknowledge that I am created in the image and likeness of God. I walk with confidence as I allow this truth to shine forth as who I am in everything I do.

Step 3
Power in Relationships

The beauty, the opportunity, and the key to happiness and joy in relationships is how you respond and react to everything. Everything - meaning the so-called good and the so-called bad. You are in a position of choice. Choice is a demonstration of your ultimate spiritual authority in the physical world of effects.

1. Life is lived from the inside out. Your thoughts are the seeds planted in the garden of your mind. Whatever thoughts you plant in your mind will grow into your life's experience.
2. You can never control what others do but you can control how you think about it and how you respond to what happens.
3. The experience of your relationship begins with you. Taking responsibility for what you are choosing is a spiritually mature action.

Choice: Your Ultimate Authority

When you understand that your partner's actions reflect *their* thoughts and beliefs, you no longer take what they do personally. They are being who they are the best way that they know in the moment.

- Who will you be in response to what is occurring?
- Will you choose to have an open caring heart or will you choose to see yourself as a victim?

Having an open heart does not mean you are a doormat. You are not required to let anyone treat you badly. You can choose to look at what is occurring and make a choice that serves your life.

I accept and know that I have been given the power of choice in every situation and every circumstance. I choose to see from a place of love and compassion that empowers me to live a life of grace, spiritual understanding, and joy.

Step 4
What Is Love?

You learn about love through observation and experiences in your life and cultural norms that are broadcast through movies, songs and adopted by society. This makes it very likely you will embrace popular understandings about love. However; your beliefs about love, where it is, how to get it, and how to keep it will determine your experience of love and loving.

1. Love is not something you get or earn from another. Love is a quality of God- eternal, unchanging, unfolding, and it has no opposites. It just is.
2. Love is the essence of life and living. Love, like God, is present everywhere.
3. Love is limitless and love is WHO YOU ARE! You don't have to seek it from another because it is present in and as your life.

Love: A Journey of Self-Discovery

Love is a spiritual truth. It encourages you to love others as you love yourself freely, openly and without judgement. Just as water is wet, and fire is hot, love is a force that is present and always available. Anything unlike love will reveal itself as an opportunity to return to love's path of wholeness.

- If you are not aware of love as who you are, you will seek it in another and become disappointed and heartbroken when it doesn't work.
- No one can give or take love from you because love is essentially who you are.

Love is always encouraging you to discover Its truth. Search your heart to discover love at the center of your being. Like a magnet, the love that you are radiates and attracts love in your life experiences.

I call forward the love that resides and lives at the center of my being. I effortlessly step forward into this truth and I live my life radiating the warmth, the brilliance and the magnificence of love that is a beacon of light in the world.

Step 5
Relationships Require More Than Love

Love is essential in relationships. Just as a house needs a foundation to stand, love is the foundation of a relationship. However, the house is not complete if there is only a foundation. Relationships definitely need love but they require more than love to thrive.

1. Practicing spiritual qualities like openness, forgiveness, joy, humor, understanding, and compassion play a part in keeping a relationship viable and strong.
2. Many couples deeply love each other but they cannot make the relationship work because they lack the ability grow in the qualities that are essential to a relationship's success.

What Will You Do for Love?

Allowing yourself to be conscious and aware of what a relationship requires to thrive gives you an opportunity to grow and expand those essential qualities in your life.

- Be honest with yourself on the spiritual qualities where you shine and where you need to grow.
- Be willing to open your heart and lovingly allow yourself to accept an expanded understanding of those spiritual qualities you need to anchor in your relationship.
- Set an intention to allow those qualities to grow in your life.

Lovingly I allow the grace of God to lead and guide me towards opening my heart to be a person where love thrives as compassion, forgiveness, joy, and goodness in my life and in my relationships. I am thankful and grateful that I am growing and expanding to be a greater place where love can shine in the world.

Step 6
Relationships Inside Out

You may think a relationship is building a loving connection with another person. That is an outcome of relationship, but in order to have that outcome you must first have a healthy relationship with yourself. You tend to be attracted to who you are and what you think you deserve.

1. In reality the first relationship you have is with yourself. You are your primary relationship.
2. How you are with you is how others will learn to be with you. If you feel unworthy, you will attract someone who confirms that to you.
3. Examine how you treat and take care of yourself. How do you think about yourself? Are you considerate and caring of yourself?
4. Everything you want someone to do and be for you, you must do and be for yourself.
5. Fall in love with yourself, a love that allows you to see the beauty and love in yourself that can transfer to others.

It Begins with You

Become a loving presence in your own life. Take care of yourself emotionally and physically. Eat well. Take time to have fun. Rest and recover when you have worked hard. Forgive yourself when you make a mistake and praise yourself for the wonderful things you do in life.

- Being confident and caring is attractive to others.
- Being comfortable in your skin projects a positive energy that makes people want to be in your space.
- Respect and honor yourself and others will respect and honor you.

I take this time to love and honor myself. I am worthy of my care and my attention. I am considerate of my needs and my wants. I recognize my gifts and the unique way I participate in life and living. As I recognize and acknowledge my worth, I recognize and acknowledge the worth of others. I am available to share the goodness of my life in a loving, caring relationship.

Step 7
Relationships: A Reason, A Season or A Lifetime

Relationships can last for short or long periods of time. You can be with one person for a lifetime, for a period of time, or you may have short relationships with many people during your life. All relationships have a shelf life and they occur for either a reason, a season or a lifetime.

1. When relationships happen for a reason you may learn a lesson about yourself, your life or love in a short period of time. After you learn what the relationship offers it seems to lose its reason for being and you find that it dissolves.
2. Relationships for a season do the same thing as relationships for a reason but they will last longer period of time, maybe even years.
3. Relationships for a lifetime experience the ups and downs and lessons of relationships but there is something that holds the couple together through all of the changes.
4. Whatever your soul needs to learn through relationships will be learned no matter how long it takes.

A Reason, A Season, A Lifetime

It is important to use spiritual discernment, not fear, to determine if the relationship has run its course. If you are always having the same issue in relationships that is a signal that you have something you haven't learned and the question is, will you learn it now, or later?

- Open your awareness to Divine Intuitive Wisdom that lives in you and ask questions on the status of your relationship.
- Remain open to receive information beyond your opinions, fears, anger and expectations.

Every relationship, no matter how long it lasts has value for you and your experience of love and loving. Open your inner eye to the gifts the relationship brings.

I use spiritual discernment to inform me on the actions and direction I should take for my relationship. I trust that Divine Intuitive Wisdom is present and available and I am grateful that it lovingly supports me in living a life of joy and love.

Step 8
Inner Knowing: What Am I Pretending Not to Know ?

A powerful question to ask yourself is, "What am I pretending not to know?" The key word is "pretending". You have Divine Intuitive Wisdom that is always available and aware of energy and information not present to your conscious, rational, intellectual mind.

1. In other words, you are divinely designed with the ability to tap into infinite knowledge and wisdom that is always present.
2. You are equipped with Divine Intuitive Wisdom that works like preloaded software. It is your Cosmic GPS.
3. You have always used this energy in your life when you get a feeling or a hunch about something or someone.
4. To access your Divine Intuitive Wisdom you need to slow down, tune in and BE OPEN. Become aware of the unique way Divine Intuitive Wisdom shows up for you in your life.

Cosmic GPS: Your Ally in Relationships

Your Intuitive Inner Wisdom becomes your ally with the complexities of relationships.

- It leads and guides you to determine the direction and course of action you should take in a relationship and in your life.
- Dedicate time, even five minutes per day to be still and become aware of how it communicates to you.

Acknowledging and checking in with your Inner Wisdom is not cosmic bubble wrap that protects you from all bad things in life.

- Trusting and accessing your Divine Intuitive Wisdom allows you to be self-assured and confident that whatever you need to know is available to you.

I know that right where I am there is a loving power and a presence available to me that informs, guides, and directs me. I turn my attention to this presence and I listen with my whole heart to Its wisdom, Its love and Its guidance for my life.

Step 9
Crisis: An Opportunity in Relationships

Every relationship experiences a time when there is conflict. Sometimes the conflict is manageable and small and other times it is a crisis that shakes the foundation of the relationship to its core. As counterintuitive as it sounds, conflict in a relationship can be productive if seen from a spiritual understanding.

1. Anything that is unlike REAL love will fail. That failure will look like conflict, issues, drama and problems.
2. Conflict has the ability to highlight unhealed patterns, wounds and misguided beliefs that need to be transformed and addressed.
3. Some unhealed patterns could be the need to be right, possessiveness, judgment, criticism, manipulation and anger just to name a few.

From Heartbreak to Breakthrough

If you look at the conflict beyond the *effect* to the *cause* it can produce an enlightened and healing understanding of what's happening. Ask yourself:

- What is the conflict trying to show me about loving?
- What lesson in this conflict serves my life?
- What belief, wound or old life pattern is surfacing as a result of this conflict?
- What am I being called to do or be as a result of this conflict?
- What higher good can be gained through this conflict?

Conflict gets your attention by disrupting your comfort. It is encouraging you to grow beyond your idea of yourself into a new way of being.

I am willing to look deeper into the events of my life to learn, to grow, and to be transformed by Spirit to be free of anything that holds me back from experiencing life to the fullest.

Step 10
Change: Who Are We Now?

Change is a permanent condition of living in the physical world. When you are in relationship expect you, your partner, and the relationship to undergo changes.

1. Some changes are visible like changes in your physical appearance.
2. Other changes will be internal and emotional based on living and experiencing life.
3. Expect the relationship to change because of the personal changes each of you may experience.
4. Expecting and wanting your partner and the relationship to never change is like wanting the ocean not to have waves. Its futile!

Practice Acceptance of Change

Acceptance is a spiritual principle that allows you to see "what is" without judgment. Acceptance allows you to stay at peace and grace while people and things are changing around you.

- Become aware of how you and your partner are changing and growing and how it is shifting the relationship.
- When you accept and are aware of the changing nature of people and relationships you can experience the spiritual quality of freedom.
- Stay aware of the spiritual principles of love, freedom and acceptance that are eternal, changeless and allow you to live in grace through the changes.

With ease and grace, I turn within to accept and experience the changing nature of my life, my partner and our relationship. I call forward a deeper understanding and an enlightened acceptance of the changes that are occurring. I know that ultimately I am being guided and supported to live my best life through, and as a result of the changes.

Step 11
Infidelity: You Did What?!

If your partner engages in infidelity it says more about them than it does about you. They have stepped out of integrity and acted contrary to their word and their agreement with you. This is time for you to become anchored in spiritual truth and remember who you are.

1. This is a friendly universe governed by a God that is a benevolent presence and only wants the best for your life.
2. God created you in Its image and likeness and out of all that God is.
3. Always remember that you are love.
4. The love that you are is what you share with another.
5. No one can take love away from you because they did not give it to you.
6. LOVE IS WHO YOU ARE!

Living in the Field of Love

In a relationship, you are experiencing a field of love that you have established with your partner when you freely and fully participate in the exchange of love that you both are.

- Recognize the love that you are and act accordingly.
- Call love's name as you. Honor it. Treasure it.
- Let love illumine and light your life as it supports you in accepting love as your true identity.

Not every act of infidelity is an end to a relationship. It could be the beginning of a new phase where you each deepen the care and commitment to each other.

I am grateful to clearly know and accept the love of God individualized as me. The love that I am cannot be diminished. It can only increase as I become aware of its presence as me. I accept loving relationships that are honoring, honest, and caring. I am open to receiving and sharing love that grows, expands and radiates warmth and a soulful connection of the heart.

Step 12
Forgiveness: It's All About You

Forgiveness is often misunderstood. You might think forgiving someone is sending the message that what they did was acceptable. This is so far from the truth. Forgiveness is about YOU being free from the pain, the upset, the anger and starting over.

1. There are times in a relationship when you will need to practice forgiveness.
2. Forgiving someone lifts the emotional weight from you and allows you to experience peace and freedom.
3. Forgiveness does not mean you agree with what happened.
4. You don't *forget* what happened but you let go the negative emotions that keep you anchored to what happened.
5. Forgiving allows you to learn the lessons the event brought and gain insight and perspective on you, your partner, and your relationship.

Steps in Forgiveness: A.R.F.T

Forgiveness is a spiritual process of letting go and giving yourself the gift of love and support. The four steps of forgiveness outlined here are (1) Acceptance, (2) Release, (3) Forgiveness, and (4) Trust.

- **A**cceptance is an emotional acceptance of your feelings about the incident. You express how you honestly feel about what happened.
- **R**elease is a mental understanding of what happened and a realization that holding on is not going to change the event.
- **F**orgiveness is the spiritual understanding that who you really are is much bigger than anything that has ever happened to you.
- **T**rust is restoring confidence in yourself and life. It reminds you that you are not a victim but are learning and growing through life's experiences.

*I am grateful that I forgive easily. I know that forgiveness clears **my** heart and **my** soul of any hurt and anger. Forgiving allows me to live a life filled with grace, love, power and joy.*

Step 13
How Do I Trust Again?

Trusting your heart and your being to someone you love is a sacred act. It is a process of opening your soul to be transformed by love's power and grace. In relationships however, there are times when trusting becomes difficult when trust has been broken, misused or misunderstood.

1. During times of broken trust, turn to spiritual understanding to give you a deeper insight into what's occurring.
2. Trusting is an inner activity of aligning yourself with Divine Intuitive Wisdom that is always present, always available, and never fails.
3. The trust you want or need from another must begin with you trusting yourself, and your connection with Spirit and how it operates in your life to lead and guide you towards your highest good.

Be Guided in Trusting

Become still and ask your Divine Intuitive Wisdom questions on the meaning, direction and significance of how to trust. You could ask:

- What were the ways you determined your partner was trustworthy?
- Be specific and list why you granted them your trust.
- How is this specific incident of broken trust informing you about how you trust yourself? Trust God? Trust life?

Trust will never be an issue for you when you understand and cultivate the activity and habit of listening and following your Divine Inner Wisdom.

I know that I am guided and directed by a power that is unfailing and always available. I place my trust in Its love, Its grace and Its goodness as my life. As I trust Its magnificence and glory, I openly and freely express divine insight and wisdom. I trust God's presence at the center of my being and I know it organizes the activities and the relationships of my life for the good of my being.

Step 14
Integrity: Your Super Power

What you believe is how you behave. How you behave is who and what you attract in your life. Who and what you attract in your life reflects what you believe. You don't get what you want, you get who you are. This is a spiritual truth.

1. Be in integrity.
2. Being in integrity is being in alignment with spiritual principles of compassion, care, truth, and honesty.
3. Integrity is a foundational quality of relationship. It establishes the tone for how the relationship will unfold.
4. Do you keep your word to yourself and others? Can you be counted on to follow through with what you said you would do? Are you honest with yourself and others?

Using Your Super Power

Being a person of integrity, you stand out as an attractive presence in the world. Like a magnet, you will attract people who are vibrating at the same level of your character and belief in life.

- Make a commitment to be a person of integrity.
- Keeping your word to yourself will assist you with keeping your word to others.
- Start with being honest and truthful with yourself.
- Take responsibility for your actions when you make a mistake.
- Integrity demonstrates your strength, character, and ability to stand tall in life with yourself and with others.
- Integrity is your super power.

I know I am attracting who I am and what I am being, so I choose to be in in integrity in my life. I choose to be honest with myself and with others. I choose to align my words with my actions. I choose to be a place of truth, compassion and love. I know I am being supported and guided by the full force of the universe in this activity and it is accomplished with ease and grace.

Step 15
Relationship Freedom: Stand in the Light

Relationships are a journey that can take you into the awakening of your soul and lead you toward greater freedom. You have the opportunity to learn at a deeper level who you are, what love is, how to love, and how to be your best self with someone in an intimate relationship.

1. When you remember that you are an individualized, unique fingerprint of God's grace you accept yourself as valuable and worthy and do not look to another person to validate or complete you.
2. You understand your worth and the worth of others.
3. You know and understand that love is who you are.
4. A spiritual understanding of your identity makes you aware that you are creating your life through choices and beliefs.
5. When things happen in your relationship, you have the choice to look beyond what's happening to discover the lesson and the learning that benefits your life.
6. Looking for the lesson and the learning in relationships allows you to never be the victim, but to live as a victor.

Enlightened Freedom

No matter what happens in your relationship you can always know that you are a place where goodness, grace, and love are present in the world through you. That is an *enlightened freedom* that allows you to live independent of situations and circumstances.

- Who you choose to be in the world is like a magnet that determines who you attract, who is attracted to you, and what you will experience.
- Remember, you are always connected to Divine Intuitive Wisdom that is always available to guide and support you in your life's experiences.
- Spiritual understanding is a daily practice. In relationships you get to be in the flow of the spiritual principles of love, forgiveness, joy compassion, beauty and intimacy.
- Choose your highest good and walk in the Light of Truth that is always available for you, if you accept it!

You've finished. Before you go…

Tweet/share that you finished this book.

Please star rate this book.

Reviews are solid gold to writers. Please take a few minutes to give us some itty bitty feedback.

ABOUT THE AUTHOR

Deborah was in relationship with her husband for thirty nine years. She says during those years she probably had five different relationships with her husband. She shares what she learned about love, the ups and downs of relationships, and how it can lead you to a greater experience of your authentic Self, your true power, and a personal relationship with God.

Deborah has a MA in Spiritual Psychology and is a licensed Spiritual Counselor who works with clients to guide them toward inspired living by examining and shifting the beliefs and actions that limit their life.

She is a teacher, a spiritual counselor, a workshop leader, a speaker and an example of how to use everything that happens in relationships to lead you to live a life of love and freedom.

If you enjoyed this Itty Bitty® book you might also like…

- **Your Amazing Itty Bitty® Fear Busting Book** – Lucetta Zaytoun

- **Your Amazing Itty Bitty® Self-Esteem Book** – Jade Elizabeth

- **Your Amazing Itty Bitty® How To Be A Woman Book** – Dr. Bunny Vreeland

And our many other Itty Bitty books available on line.

www.ingramcontent.com/pod-product-compliance
Lightning Source LLC
Chambersburg PA
CBHW061305040426
42444CB00010B/2525